# ANTS

A TRUE BOOK®

by

**Ann O. Squire**

**Children's Press®**
A Division of Scholastic Inc.

New York  Toronto  London  Auckland  Sydney
Mexico City  New Delhi  Hong Kong
Danbury, Connecticut

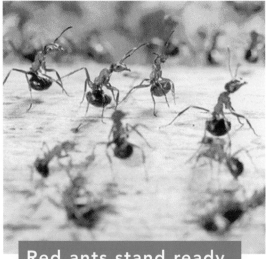

Red ants stand ready
to protect their nest.

*Reading Consultant*
**Nanci R. Vargus, Ed.D.**
*Assistant Professor*
*Literacy Education*
*University of Indianapolis*
*Indianapolis, IN*

*Content Consultant*
**Jeff Hahn**
*Department of Entomology*
*University of Minnesota*

*The photo on the cover shows
leafcutter ants transporting a
leaf. The photo on the title
page shows a black ant on a
vine in Costa Rica.*

**Dedication:**
*For Emma*

Library of Congress Cataloging-in-Publication Data

Squire, Ann.
    Ants / by Ann O. Squire
        p. cm. — (True books)
    Includes bibliographic references and index (p.  )
    ISBN 0-516-22659-2 (lib. bdg.)    0-516-29359-1 (pbk.)
    1. Ants—Juvenile literature. [1. Ants.] I. Title. II. True book.
QL568.F7 S73 2003
595.79'6—dc21

                                                        2002005881

CHILDREN'S PRESS, and A TRUE BOOK®, and associated logos are
trademarks and or registered trademarks of Scholastic Library Publishing.
SCHOLASTIC and associated logos are trademarks and or registered
trademarks of Scholastic Inc.

1 2 3 4 5 6 7 8 9 10 R 12 11 10 09 08 07 06 05 04 03

# Contents

Ants are able to carry objects that are much heavier than they are.

# The Amazing Ant

Of all the insects in the world, ants are probably the ones you think you know best. In spring and summer, ants seem to be everywhere—running along the sidewalk, getting into your picnic lunches, and even invading your kitchen. But how well do you really know ants?

Did you know that a single ant can lift an object that is fifty times its own weight? Or that it can easily climb a tree 100 feet (37 meters) high, which requires about the same effort as a person jogging to the top of Mount Everest? But the most amazing thing about ants isn't their strength, endurance, or speed. It's the fact that they work together to create huge, underground cities called

Ant colonies can have hundreds of thousands of members.

colonies that can be home to as many as one million individual ants.

These Asiatic weaver ants are just one of the many ant species that live in the jungle.

Scientists have found about ten thousand ant species, and there are many more just waiting to be discovered. Ants live all over the world, but they are most numerous in the tropics. A single tree in a tropical rain forest can be home to more than forty different ant species.

Like other insects, ants have six legs and a body that is divided into three

Ants have three body
segments and six legs.

segments. Many ants also have stingers, which isn't so surprising when you learn that ants are closely related to bees and wasps. In the 100 million years they have been on Earth, ants have changed very little. The ants scurrying down the sidewalk today are nearly identical to those that lived when dinosaurs roamed the earth!

# A Colony Is Born

Every ant colony, no matter how large, is started by a single ant. That ant is the **queen,** and her journey begins on a warm autumn day. She leaves her home and, along with many other winged females, flies high into the air to find a mate. At the same time, winged males

A queen ant will lose her wings after she mates.

also take to the air. After mating in midair, all the ants come back to the ground. Their job completed, the males soon die. But the new queen's work has just begun. After finding a suitable spot for her nest, she kicks and scrapes at her now-useless wings until they fall off. Then she tunnels deep underground, where she will spend the rest of her life laying eggs.

For many months, the queen remains all alone. She does not eat, but survives by absorbing the muscles that powered her wings. Finally, the first eggs hatch. The queen tends the **larvae** carefully, feeding them with her own saliva. Soon the larvae change into **pupae.** In this process, called **metamorphosis,**

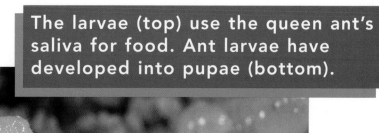

The larvae (top) use the queen ant's saliva for food. Ant larvae have developed into pupae (bottom).

Sometimes pupae wrap themselves in cocoons.

the pupae sometimes spin cocoons around themselves for protection. At the end of the pupal phase, the queen helps her daughters break out of their cocoons. They are all female

Female workers take care of larvae and pupae for the queen ant.

adult workers, ready to care for their mother and take over the work of the colony: digging tunnels, finding food, and caring for their younger sisters.

The queen continues to lay eggs, and the colony grows to

include many thousands of ants. Most of the eggs the queen lays will turn into wing-less female workers in the ever-expanding underground city. When the colony has grown large enough, she produces some sons called **drones,** as well as daughters that will become queens. The males and queens-to-be have wings, and sooner or later they will leave the colony on mating flights of their own.

# Aging Ants

Queen ants live a lot longer than their worker daughters. In fact, they live longer than almost any other insect. In the wild, most queen ants reach at least five years of age, and in captivity, they can live into their twenties. The world record is held by a black sidewalk ant, which lived to the ripe old age of twenty-nine.

Queen ants are much bigger and live much longer than their worker ants.

A black sidewalk ant can live for more than twenty years.

# Colony Life

In an ant colony, different types of work are done by different groups of ants, which are called **castes**. Ants in a particular caste are usually well suited to the kind of work they do. The leafcutter ants of South America, which gather leaves and grow underground fungus

Leafcutter ants use their largest workers to bring pieces of leaves back to the colony.

gardens, have an especially complicated caste system. Large worker ants cut leaves into pieces and bring the sections back to the colony.

Inside, slightly smaller workers cut the leaves into smaller segments. Even smaller workers mold the pieces into balls and plant them in the fungus garden. The tiniest workers of all have the job of tending the garden, sometimes pulling up clumps of fungus and carrying them out to feed their larger sisters. These miniature ants are only a bit larger than one of the commas on this page.

Very tiny workers take care of the
fungus garden in the leafcutter colony.

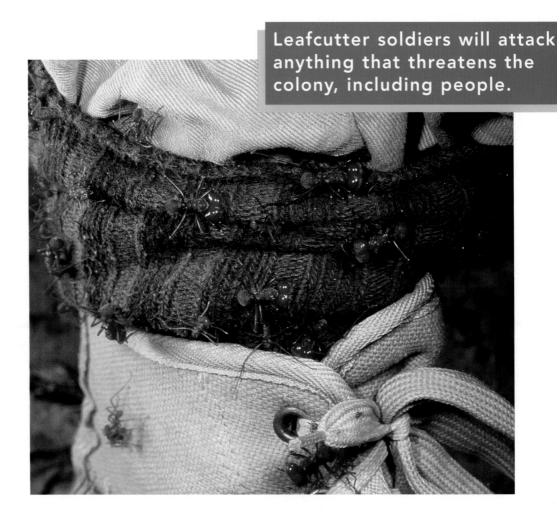

Leafcutter soldiers will attack anything that threatens the colony, including people.

On the other end of the scale are the soldiers, who have the job of defending the colony. The soldier ants can reach more than 1 inch (2.5 centimeters) in length and can weigh three hundred times as much as their gardening sisters. The giant ants use their sharp **mandibles** (jaws) not to cut leaves, but to chop their enemies into bits.

Other residents of the leafcutter ant city include the queen, whose only job is to lay eggs. The winged males in the colony do no work and are there only to reproduce with the queen.

# How Ants Communicate

Did you ever wonder how ants know when you're having a picnic? At first you see one or two ants. Then minutes later, it seems as though hundreds of ants are attacking your sandwiches. People rely on sight and sound to communicate with one another, but neither of

26

Ants quickly swarm over the food that they find.

these senses is very important to ants. They communicate by sending and receiving chemical messages.

When a hungry ant comes across a tasty picnic in progress, she grabs a sample of food and runs back toward her nest, pausing every few moments to rub her **abdomen** on the ground. By doing this, she leaves a series of scent marks that form a chemical

An ant shares the food source that it finds with others in the colony.

trail that other workers can follow to the picnic site. If she encounters any workers along the way, she may spit out a sample of the food she found for them to taste.

Ants also use chemical signals to alert each other to danger or show the location of better nesting spots. Even very young ants use chemical communication. When an egg is ready to hatch, or a new adult is ready to emerge from its

Ants will help new ants emerge from their cocoon.

cocoon, it sends out a chemical signal. Workers get the message and rush to help the young ant enter the world.

The next time you see two ants together, take a closer look. Chances are they will be touching each other or the ground with their **mouthparts** or antennae. This is how ants pick up chemical signals from each other and from their surroundings. Ants also tap or stroke one another with their antennae to send simple messages, such as "Give me a taste of that food!"

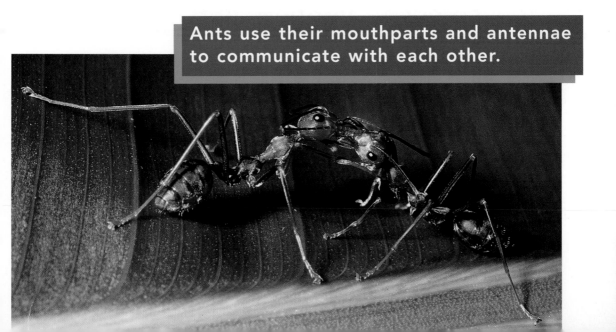

Ants use their mouthparts and antennae to communicate with each other.

# Ants at War

It has been said that humans are the most aggressive species on Earth. But when it comes to fighting, ants win the prize. One famous **myrmecologist** (a scientist who studies ants) has said that if ants had nuclear weapons, they would probably have

Ants are fierce warriors.

destroyed the world within
a week!

Most ant battles occur over
territory or food. If one type
of ant ventures too close to

another species' nest, or if two colonies discover a single food source, the result can be an all-out war.

Ants have many styles of combat. They may fight "hand to hand," wrestling with their opponents and biting off body parts with their sharp mandibles. They may spray each other with poison or use chemical weapons to drive their enemies underground. One ant species intimidates

Ants often bite off their enemy's body parts (left). Some ants can spray poisonous chemicals at their enemies (below).

Some types of ants will invade the nest holes of other ants.

opponents by dropping small pebbles into their nest holes. There is even an ant that can commit suicide to destroy its enemies. This ant, which lives in the rain forests of Malaysia, has two huge, poison-filled glands running the length of its body, turning it into a walk-ing bomb. When attacked, the ant squeezes its abdominal muscles, bursting open the sides of its body and spraying the enemy with poison.

# Some Really Amazing Ants

Army ants are some of the world's strangest—and scariest—insects. Marching across the forest floor in huge swarms, these **carnivorous** ants kill and eat everything in their path. Even large animals like elephants, monkeys, and

Army ants can quickly swarm over their victim and kill it.

humans are potential prey for these sharp-jawed ants. When night falls, the army ant swarm pauses to rest. Instead of retreating to an underground nest, the ants link their legs together to form a living shelter out of their own bodies.

Amazon ants are also fearless aggressors, but when they go on a raid, they are not looking for food. These ants invade the nests of other

An Amazon ant is very aggressive.

ant species and kidnap the
pupae, which grow up to
become the Amazons'
slaves. Why do they do this?

Amazon ants have large mouthparts for fighting.

The Amazons are not lazy. They simply cannot live without help from others.

Amazon ants are perfectly designed for war, with long, pointed mandibles. Unfortunately, those jaws are useless for doing everyday work, such as gathering food, cleaning a nest, and caring for delicate eggs and larvae. All of this work must be done by the slaves, without whom the fierce Amazons could not survive.

# To Find Out More

If you'd like to learn more about ants, check out these additional resources.

 **Books**

Holldobler, Bert and Edward O. Wilson. **Journey to the Ants.** Belknap Press of Harvard University Press, 1994.

Mason, Herbert Molloy. **The Fantastic World of Ants.** New York, NY: David McKay Company, 1974.

Miller, Sara Swan. **Ants, Bees, and Wasps of North America** (Animals in Order). Danbury, CT: Franklin Watts, 2003.

Pascoe, Elaine. **Ants** (Nature Close-Up). Woodbridge, CT: Blackbirch Press, 1998.

# Organizations and Online Sites

**Insecta Inspecta**

*http://www.insecta-inspecta.com*

More information on Argentine ants, army ants, red fire ants, and leafcutter ants.

**Myrmecology**

*http://www.myrmecology.org*

Lots of information about the study of ants, plus instructions for building a variety of ant farms.

# Important Words

*abdomen* the rear part of an insect's body

*carnivorous* meat eating

*caste* a group of ants that performs a particular function in the colony

*drone* a male ant, bee, or wasp

*larva* an insect at its first stage of development after coming out of the egg and before becoming a pupa

*mandible* jaw

*metamorphosis* the change in form that insects go through as they develop

*mouthparts* structures near an insect's mouth that are adapted for gathering food

*myrmecologist* a scientist who studies ants

*pupa* the stage in an insect's life between the larval and adult stages

*queen* the reproductive female ant that lays eggs and produces offspring

# Index

# Meet the Author

Ann O. Squire has a Ph.D. in animal behavior. Before becoming a writer, she spent several years studying African electric fish and the special signals they use to communicate with each other. Dr. Squire is the author of many books on animals and natural science topics, including *Seashells*, *Fossils*, *Animal Homes*, and *Animal Babies*. She lives with her children, Emma and Evan, in Katonah, New York.

Photographs © 2003: Bruce Coleman Inc./George D. Dodge: 41, 42; Dwight R. Kuhn Photography: 13, 15 top, 15 bottom, 16, 19 bottom; Minden Pictures/Mark W. Moffett: 21, 23, 24, 28, 30, 33, 35 top, 36; Peter Arnold Inc./Hans Pfletschinger: 2, 35 bottom, 39; Photo Researchers, NY: 31 (Dr. Ivan Polunin), 1 (Gary Retherford), 19 top (J.H. Robinson), 7 (Kenneth Thomas); Robert & Linda Mitchell: cover, 8, 10, 17; Visuals Unlimited: 27 (D. Newman), 4 (Kjell Sandved).